# THiS BOOK BELONGS TO

..............................................

# COLOR TEST PAGE

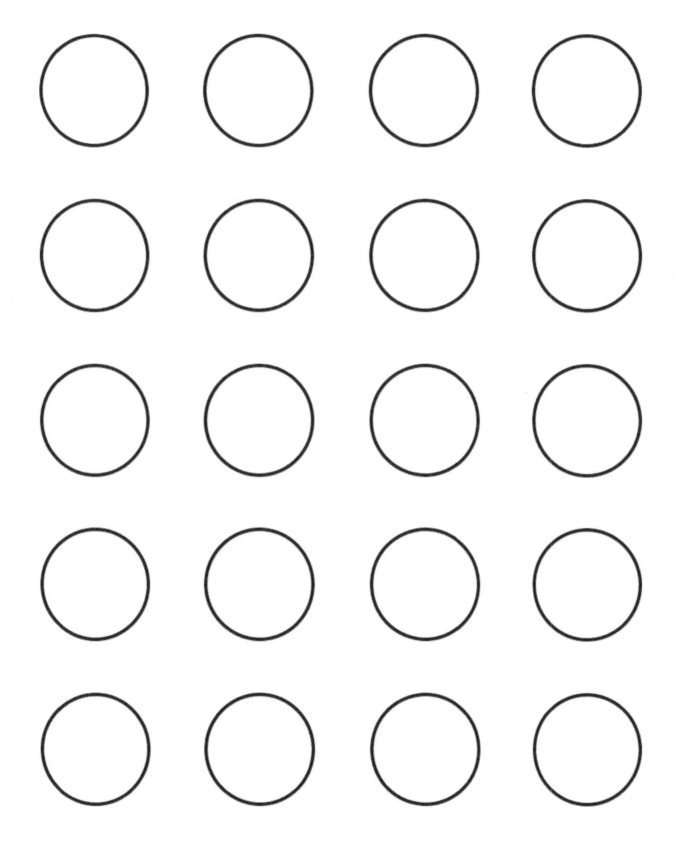

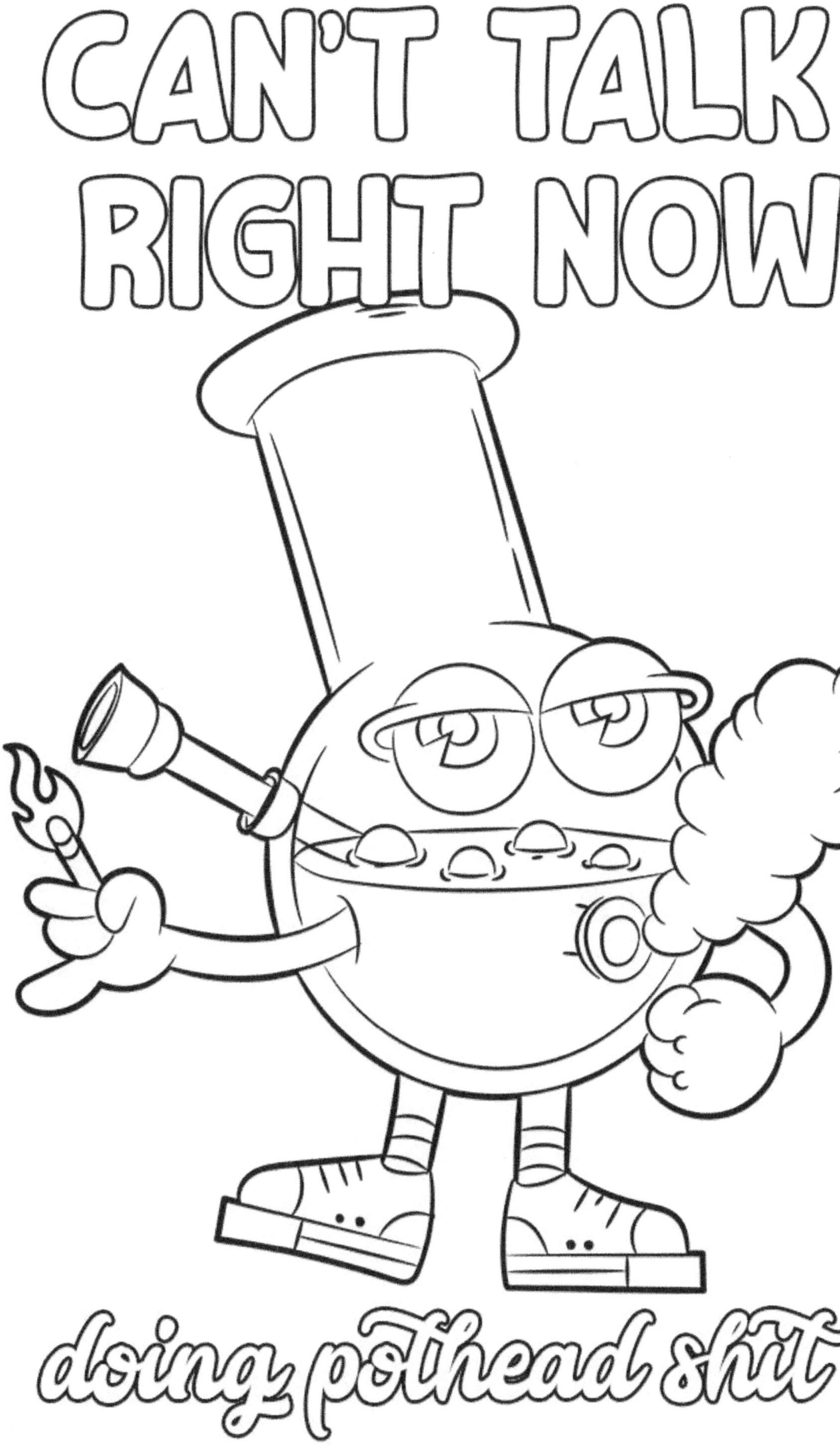
CAN'T TALK
RIGHT NOW
doing pothead shit

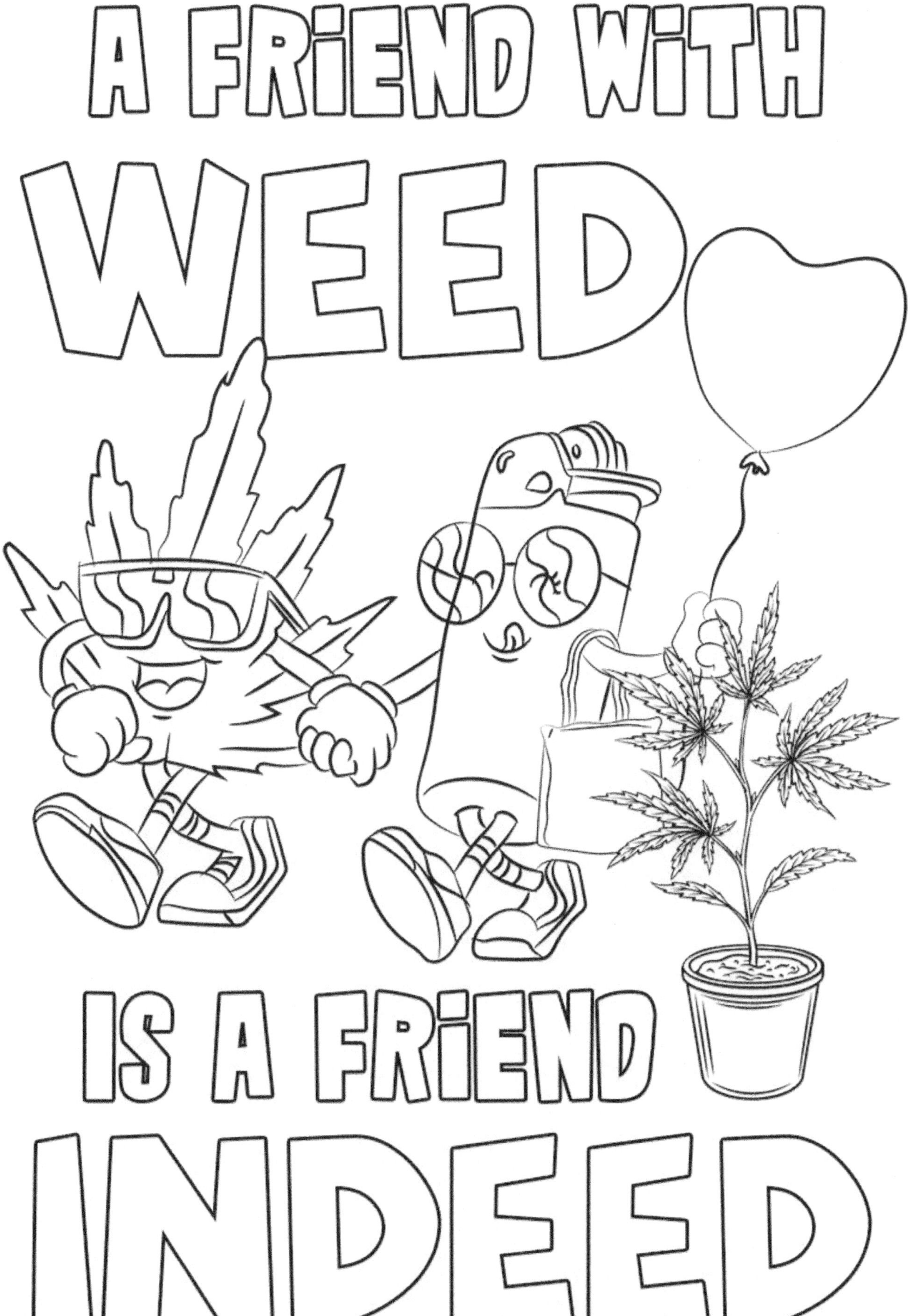
A FRIEND WITH
WEED
IS A FRIEND
INDEED

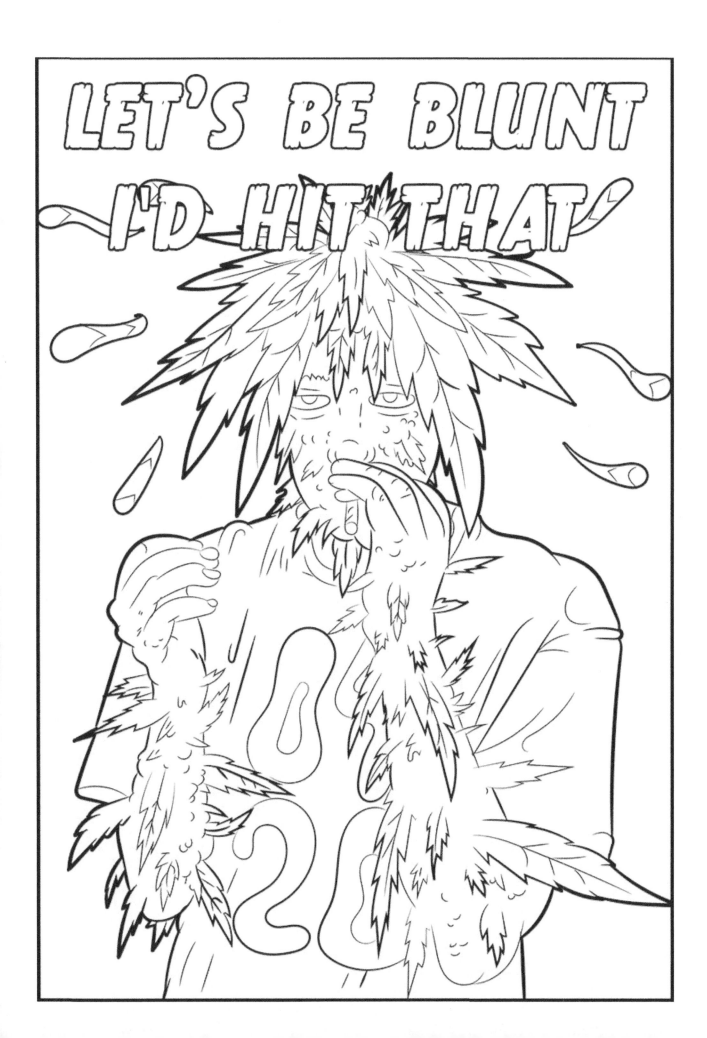

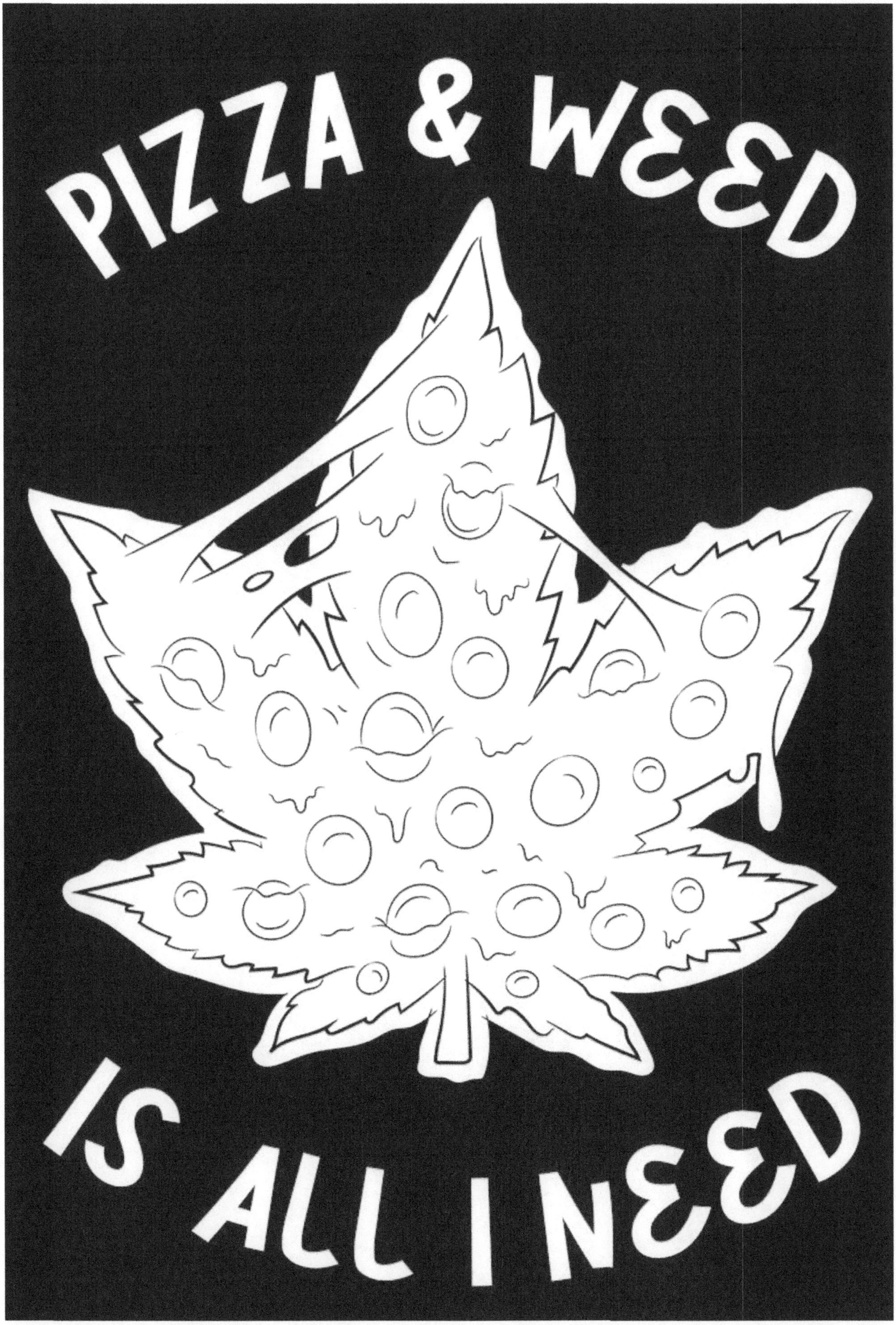
PIZZA & WEED
IS ALL I NEED

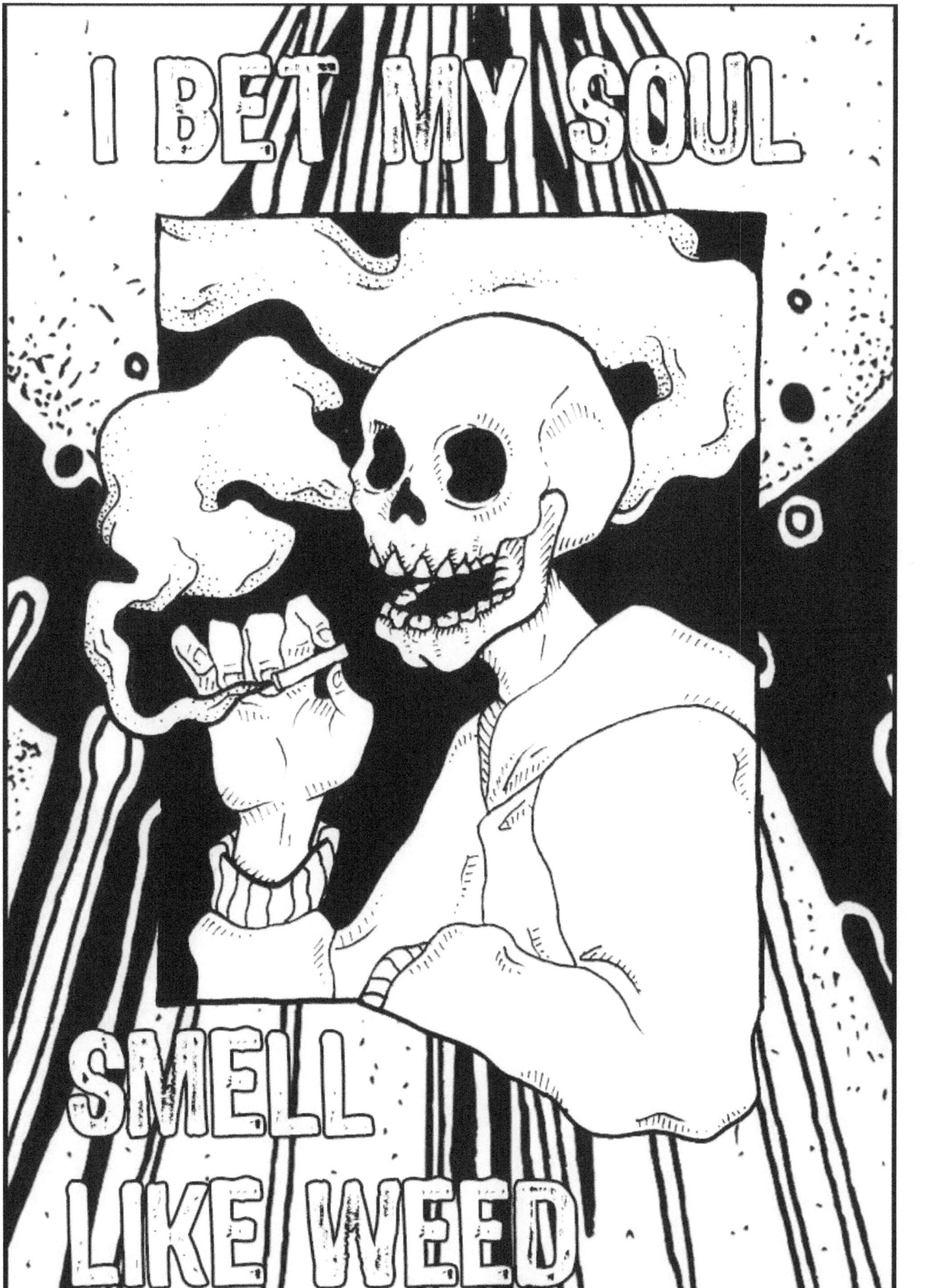
I BET MY SOUL
SMELL
LIKE WEED

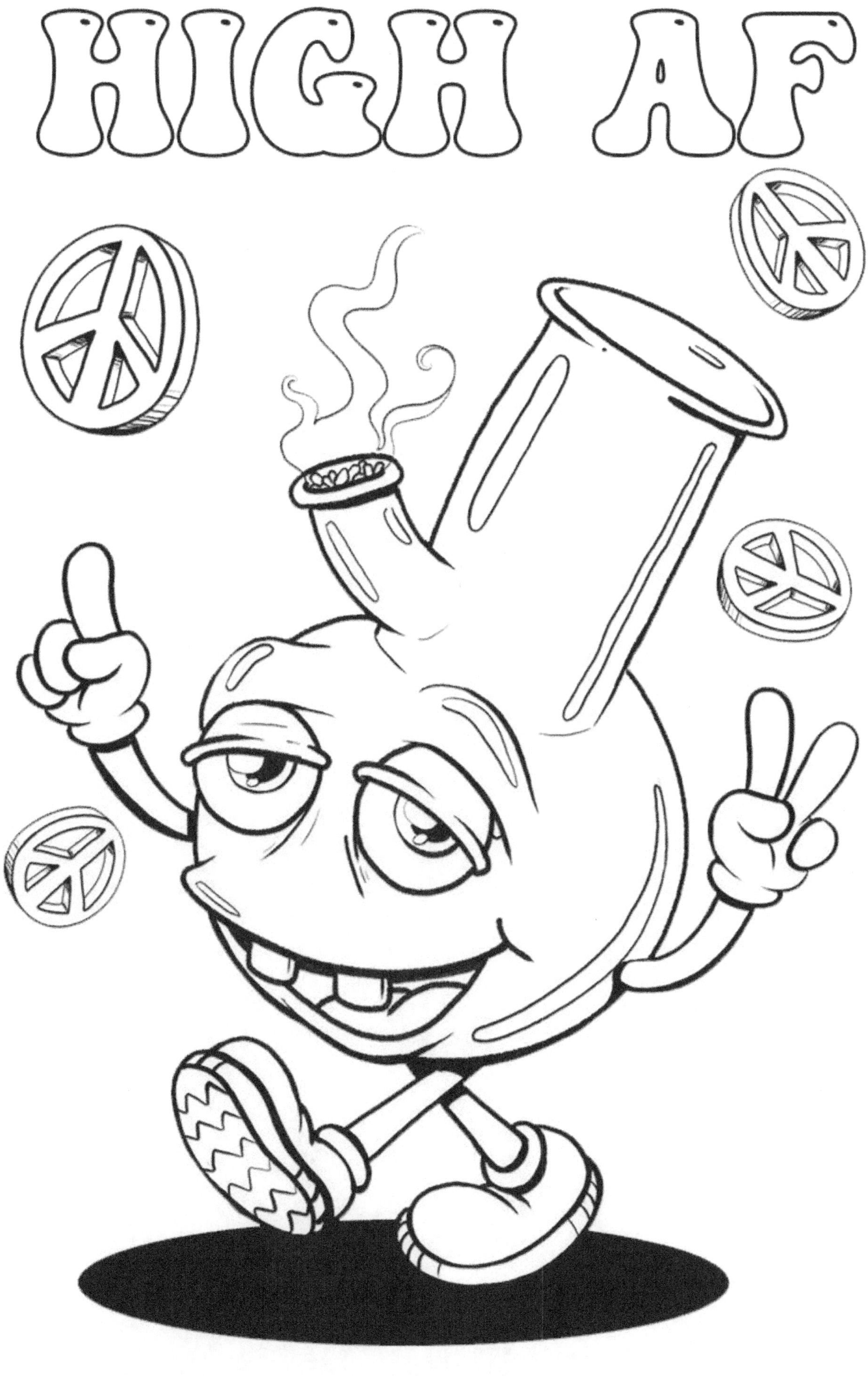
HIGH AF

# HIGH AS A KITE

# MIDNIGHT TOKER

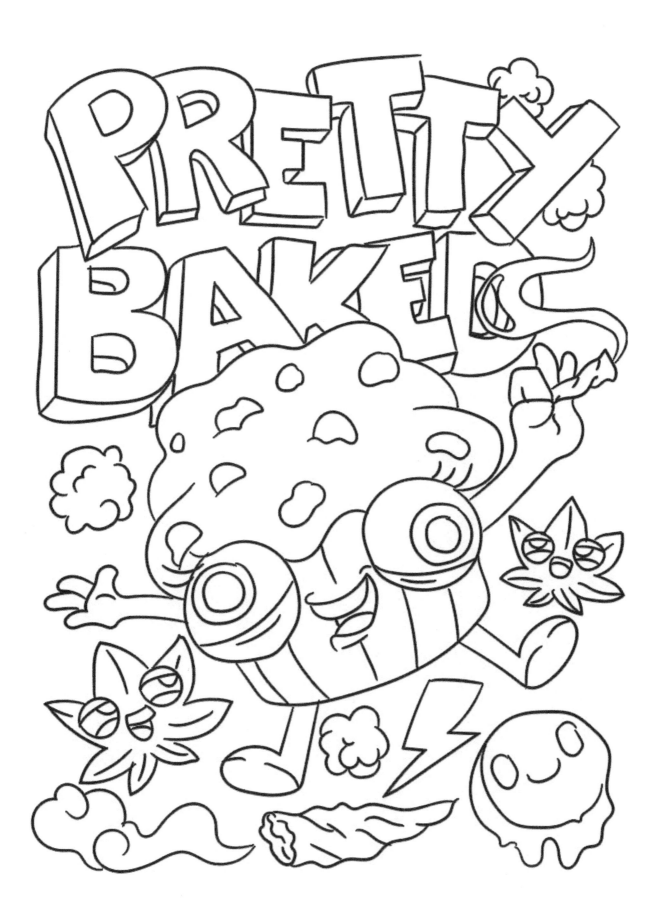

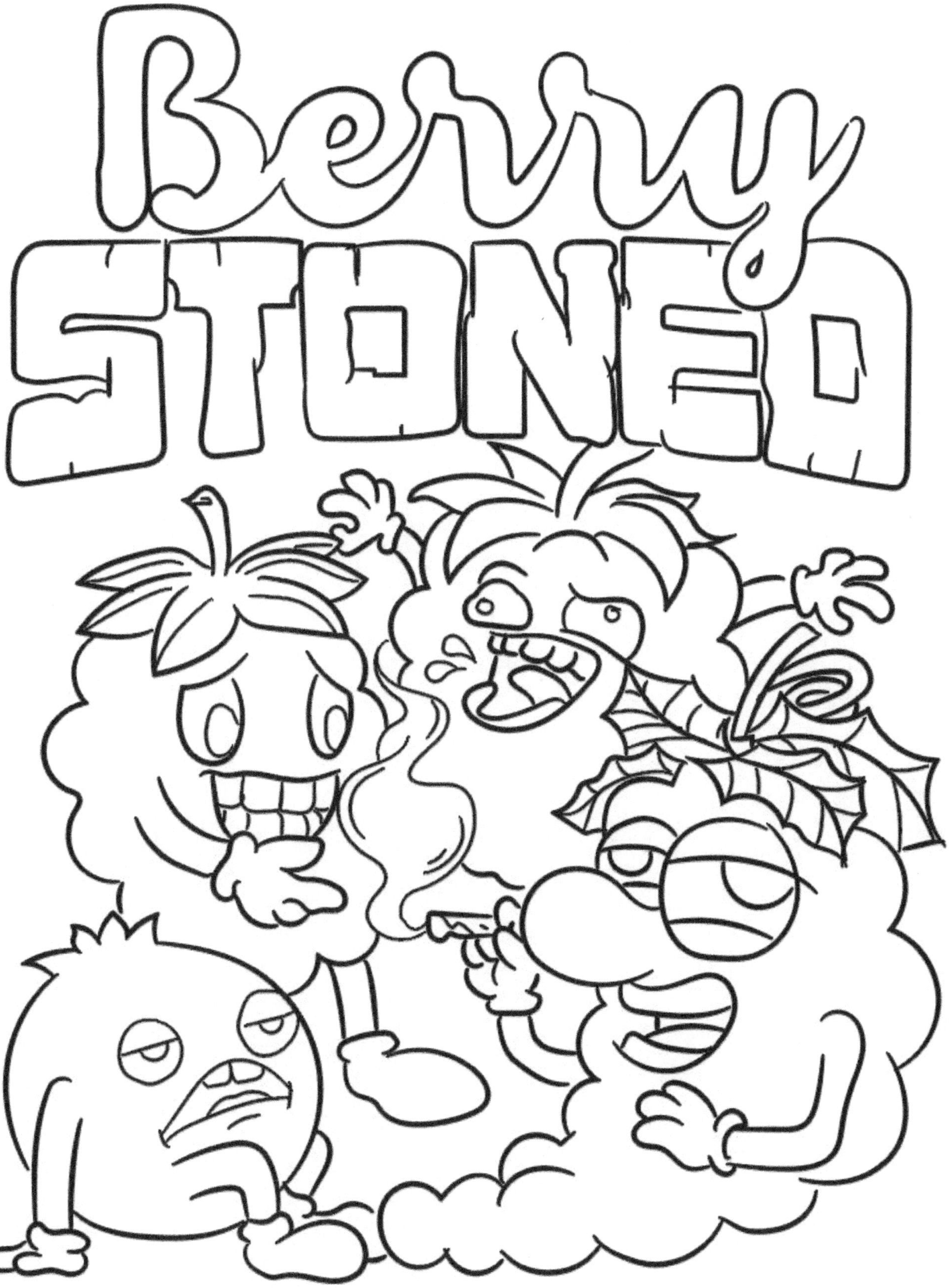
Berry
STONED

# BAKE & CAKE

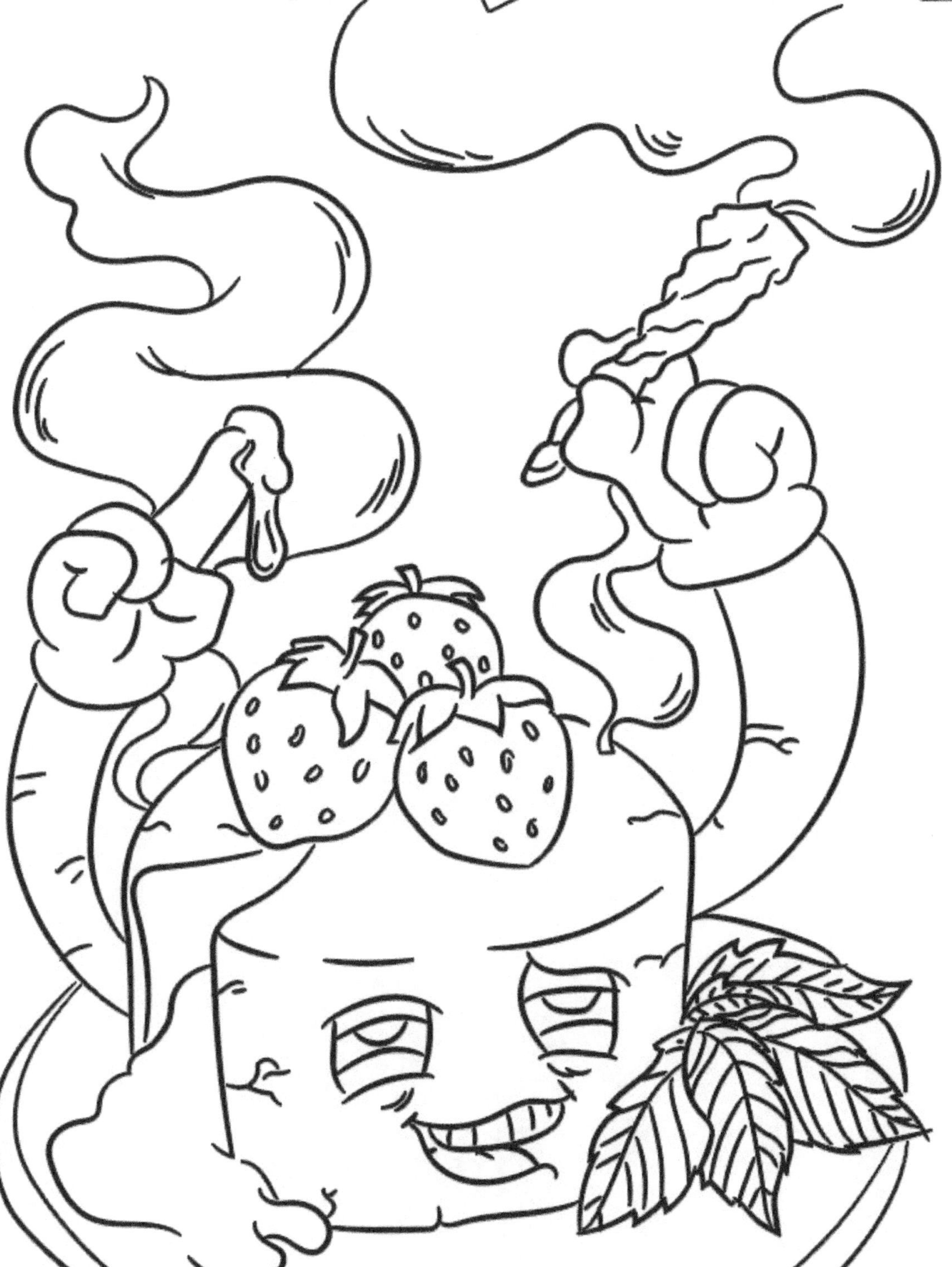

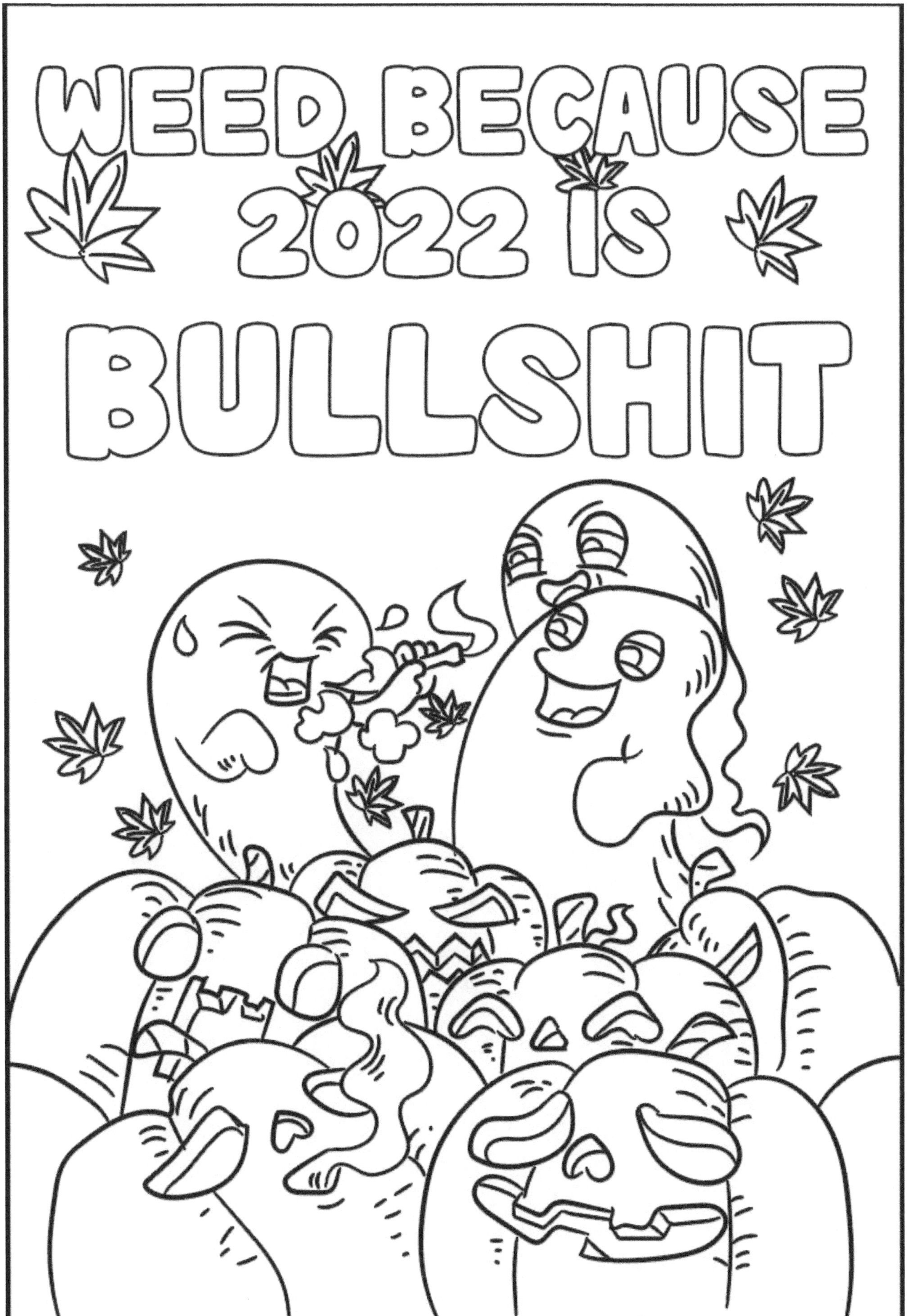
WEED BECAUSE
2022 IS
BULLSHIT

# HOW WAS YOUR COLORING EXPERIENCE?

Let us know in a review on Amazon!
( Hint hint: We get so happy when we see photos and videos of your talented artist work! We'd be thrilled if you include a photo or video in your review)

Made in the USA
Las Vegas, NV
16 September 2024

95369516R00046